Achieving Immutability Patterns in JavaScript

Table of Contents

Chapter 1. Introduction

Welcome to this Special Report detailing a crucial and fascinating realm of JavaScript: achieving immutability patterns. This topic, while quite technical, is thoroughly broken down into digestible pieces, allowing for seamless assimilation of knowledge irrespective of your proficiency level. This report delves into the heart of JavaScript, providing critical insights into making your applications more predictable and easier to debug via immutability. Whether you are a seasoned developer or an enthusiastic beginner aiming to grasp the ropes of an exciting, in-demand and dynamic language like JavaScript, this report is sure to augment your skills and stimulate your coding journey. A mastery of immutability promises elegance, power, and control over your codebase, making it an imperative achievement in your JavaScript adventure. Buy this special report today and embark on unlocking JavaScript's full potential.

Chapter 2. Understanding Immutability in JavaScript

To delve into the concept of Immutability in JavaScript, we first need to understand what immutability is and why it's essential. Immutability is a principle of keeping data unchanging over time or unable to be changed. It's a core concept in functional programming, and it's becoming more prevalent in other paradigms due to the development of libraries/frameworks like React/Redux, which heavily rely on this principle.

2.1. The Problem with Mutability

Data alteration, or mutation, is a common operation in any programming language. In JavaScript, altering data can be problematic. Due to its dynamic nature, JavaScript allows direct modification of an object's properties or an array. This behavior can lead to confusing code, making it harder to debug applications. For instance, if you pass an object to a function and modify it there, the modifications affect the original object outside the function.

```
let obj = {name: "John"};
let modifyObj = function(o) {
  o.name = "Jane";
};
modifyObj(obj);
console.log(obj); // Outputs {name : "Jane"}
```

In this example, we expected the `obj` to stay the same, but it was actually modified.

2.2. Achieving Immutability for Basic Data Types

For basic data types like Number, String, Boolean, Null, and Undefined, JavaScript follows immutability by default. When you create a variable, the value is directly stored in the variable. Upon changing it, a new memory space is created for the new value.

```
let a = 1;
let b = a;
b = 2;
console.log(a); // Outputs 1
console.log(b); // Outputs 2
```

In this case, even though the value of b is changed, the variable a remains the same.

2.3. Achieving Immutability for Objects and Arrays

JavaScript's default behavior for complex data types (Objects, Arrays) differs; they are mutable. When you assign an object or array to a variable, JavaScript stores a reference to the object, not the actual object. It can result in inadvertently affecting the object elsewhere in the code, causing unexpected results or data corruption.

To prevent these issues, we aim to adopt Immutability for Objects and Arrays.

1. *Creating a Shallow Copy*

One way is to create a shallow copy of the original object. Any number of modifications to the copy will not impact the original object.

```
let arr = [1, 2, 3];
let arrCopy = arr.slice();
arrCopy[0] = 'a';
console.log(arr); // Outputs [1, 2, 3]
console.log(arrCopy); // Outputs ['a', 2, 3]
```

The `slice()` method copies all elements of the array into a new one, but it creates a shallow or surface level copy. That means if your array or object contains other arrays or objects, they won't be recreated; only references to them will be copied.

1. *Deep Copying*

Clone an object recursively, copying every property's value into a new object. This avoids references to the original nested items.

```
let obj={
  name:'John',
  address: {
    street: '123 XYZ St'
  }
}
let newObj = JSON.parse(JSON.stringify(obj));
newObj.address.street = '456 ABC Rd';
console.log(obj.address.street); // Outputs '123 XYZ St'
console.log(newObj.address.street); // Outputs '456 ABC
Rd'
```

In this case, `JSON.parse(JSON.stringify(obj))` is used to deep clone an object.

Please note, this is a quick and simple way to deep clone an object, but it has its limitations: it will not correctly copy object's with functions, Dates, or RegExps properties.

2.4. Immutable Data Structures

Immutable data structures are another way to achieve immutability. Libraries like Immutable.js or immer provide such structures. Once created, these data structures cannot be changed and ensure that every mutation will result in a new instance.

2.5. Debugging Made Easier with Immutability

Having immutable data holds several advantages, one of which is reduced complexity when debugging applications. Since data cannot be changed, there's no need to track changes to a variable, making tracing bugs much simpler.

2.6. Conclusion

Immutability in JavaScript is a practical programming practice that, when properly implemented, makes your code cleaner, safer, and easier to comprehend. It might come with its complexities for complex data types but adopting strategies like copying or using immutable data structures can alleviate these challenges. Even though initially it may seem a tad bit cumbersome, the long-term benefits it offers make it an invaluable tool in a programmer's toolkit.

Chapter 3. The Role of Immutability in Functional Programming

Immutability and functional programming go hand in hand. Both are firmly rooted in mathematics, particularly in Lambda Calculus, which is a fundamental component of computation theory. The quintessence of functional programming revolves around treating computation as the evaluation of mathematical function and avoiding changing state and mutable data.

3.1. The Premise of Immutability

Immutability in its simplest form means 'unchanging over time' or 'unable to be changed'. In the sphere of programming, and in the context of JavaScript, an immutable object is an object whose state cannot be modified after it is created. This concept is in stark contrast with mutable data, which is a data structure that can be altered or modified.

Understanding these two concepts helps create a bridge to acknowledging the role of immutability in functional programming. At its core, immutability restricts any change to the data after its creation, a principle that syncs well with functional applications of JavaScript.

This paradigm of functional programming, when one chooses to follow it, bestows the tremendous advantage of preventing side effects, thus aiding in the production of more predictable, reliable, and easier-to-debug applications.

3.2. Immutability: Pillar of Functional Programming

Functional programming is popular for its breezy debugging experience and the notion of writing cleaner and more maintainable code. This all becomes possible due to the non-destructive behavior of functional languages supported through immutability.

The crux of this behavior is ensuring that functions have no impact beyond their scope and their return value. Hence, a function's output is dependent only on the input, providing a deterministic experience. This concept is known as "pure" functions. And purity, in this context, is maintained through immutability.

Fundamentally, in functional JavaScript, we pass around values. Those values should be immutable to ensure the operation's safety, limiting the origin of tricky bugs that mutate data and cause chaos in your code.

3.3. Encouraging Immutability in JavaScript

JavaScript, by default, does not enforce immutability. Built-in primitives such as strings and numbers are immutable by nature, however, objects and arrays, which are often used to handle related data, are mutable. This means that these data structures can have their properties altered even after the initial declaration. This behavior is handy when you want to keep data in sync across different parts of the application, but it also opens doors for some unexpected bugs due to their mutability.

To enforce immutability for objects and arrays in JavaScript, you have several options. Tools such as `Object.freeze()`, `Object.seal()`, and `Object.preventExtensions()` are among the built-in methods to prevent changes to objects. On the other hand, arrays can be treated as immutable subjects by applying non-mutating methods and strategies such as using the spread (···) syntax or the `Array.prototype.concat()` method.

Advanced libraries, such as Immutable.js from Facebook, provide many persistent immutable data structures including `List`, `Stack`, `Map`, `OrderedMap`, `Set`, `OrderedSet`, and `Record`. These data structures are highly efficient and designed to complement JavaScript's standard mutable data structures.

3.4. Advantages and Challenges of Immutability

Implementing immutability provides a host of advantages.

1. Predictability: Since data cannot be changed once created, the code is more predictable and easier to understand. When functions cannot alter any outside state, it's simpler to follow the flow of data throughout your program.

2. Debugging: As the state does not change, debugging becomes significantly simpler. You know exactly where, when, and why your data is the way it is.

3. Performance Optimization: Immutable data structures allow you to make efficient comparisons between the previous and current state, an advantage leveraged by libraries such as React.js for efficient re-rendering of components.

4. Concurrency: Immutable data can be read and processed by multiple threads simultaneously without the risk of data conflicts.

On the flip side, immutability does present challenges as well.

1. Memory Overhead: Updating data means copying it, which can

be a memory hit, especially with large data structures.

2. Cognitive Overhead: Thinking in terms of immutable data and pure functions can be a steep turn from procedural and OO programming.

3. Compatibility Issues: Many JavaScript libraries and patterns are written with mutability in mind. Working around these limitations can sometimes cause difficulty.

3.5. Conclusion

In conclusion, immutability is a core principle of functional programming that enables developers to write safer, cleaner, and more maintainable code. JavaScript does not enforce immutability but provides several tools, techniques, and libraries to ensure that developers can harness its power to build efficient and reliable applications. Despite a few challenges, the benefits of embracing immutability are multi-fold, making it an essential tool in any serious JavaScript programmer's toolkit.

As functional programming principles continue to be adopted by JavaScript and its community, the concept of immutability is only likely to become more crucial in the realm of JavaScript. It will continue to shape the way we think about data flow, about function purity, and about writing code that can stand the test of time.

Chapter 4. The Concept of Mutable and Immutable Objects

In object-oriented and functional programming, the concept of mutable and immutable objects play a crucial role in determining how we interact with data storage and manipulation. Understanding this fundamental characteristic of objects is crucial while working with a dynamic language like JavaScript.

Firstly, an object in the context of JavaScript refers to a standalone entity with properties and types. It's like a container holding related data and functionality. An object can represent a person with a name property, methods can be assigned to objects, and these methods represent the behaviour of an object.

Chapter 5. Understanding Mutable Objects

Mutable objects are those objects whose state or value can be changed after it is created. Most objects in JavaScript are mutable. For instance, when you create an object, you can later modify its properties or add new properties to it.

```javascript
let person = { name: "Alice", age: 40 };
console.log(person.name); // Alice

// mutating the name
person.name = "Bob";
console.log(person.name); // Bob
```

In this example, we created an object named `person`. Later in the process, we changed the `name` property of this `person` object, hence mutating it.

Chapter 6. Beware of Mutating Shared Objects

Mutable objects become problematic when they are shared or referenced in multiple places. Let's look at an example:

```
let person1 = { name: "Alice", age: 40 };
let person2 = person1;

// mutate person1
person1.name = "Bob";
console.log(person2.name); // Bob
```

In the above example, `person2` is referencing the same object as `person1`. Hence, when `person1` is mutated, the change is reflected in `person2` as well.

Chapter 7. Understanding Immutable Objects

Immutable objects, on the other hand, are those objects whose state or value cannot be changed once they are created. Numbers, strings, null, undefined, and booleans are primitive types in JavaScript and are immutable.

Once a string or a number or any other primitive type is created, we cannot change its state. Consider the following example:

```
let message = "Hello";
message[1] = "a";
console.log(message);  //Hello
```

Even though we attempted to replace the second character of the message, it remains unchanged. This demonstrates that strings are immutable in JavaScript.

Chapter 8. When are Immutables not so Immutable?

Things tend to get a bit tricky when we discuss objects and immutability because JavaScript's objects are not truly immutable. But we can achieve immutability in JavaScript objects through certain methods.

In more common scenarios, it's useful to prevent mutation in our JavaScript code to make it easier to trace and debug errors, to predict code behavior, and to avoid side effects.

Chapter 9. Making JavaScript Objects Immutable

Arrays and objects are mutable in JavaScript. However, there are a few ways to make them immutable:

9.1. Using Object.freeze()

JavaScript provides this method, which can be used to make an object immutable. When an object is frozen, you can't add new properties to it, can't delete properties from it, and can't change its existing properties or method.

```
let employee = { name: "Alice", designation: "Developer"
};
Object.freeze(employee);

employee.name = "Bob";  // Will not have any effect
console.log(employee.name); // Alice
```

The `freeze()` method has its shortcomings. It's shallow, not deep. This means that only the top layer is made immutable. If it's an object of objects, the lower level objects can be modified. However, you can recursively freeze each object to handle this.

9.2. Using the Spread Syntax

Another way to achieve immutability in JavaScript is by using the spread syntax (...). The spread operator creates a new object or array, enabling the original data structure to remain unmutated.

```javascript
let employee = { name: "Alice", designation: "Developer"
};
let newEmployee = { ...employee, name: "Bob" };

console.log(employee.name); // Alice
console.log(newEmployee.name); // Bob
```

In this example, even though the `name` property was changed for the `newEmployee` object, the `employee` object remained unmutated.

Chapter 10. Final Thoughts

In JavaScript, understanding mutability can be a double-edged sword. It allows us to keep data consistent across multiple shared references, making our apps easier to debug and reason about. Balancing between mutable and immutable data is key to mastering JavaScript.

Building your capacity to execute both concepts appropriately will hugely influence the robustness of your coding, and the complexity of your deployed applications. Hence, understanding these JavaScript specifics becomes crucial for every coding enthusiast seeking to master the language. It makes your work more efficient, readable and robust, especially when employed diligently.

Remember, immutability is not a rule one must follow in every circumstance, but rather a tool to help keep your code predictable, easy to debug, keeping it performant in a highly interactive user interface, and hence more maintainable. The decision is yours to incorporate a level of immutability in your style of coding.

Chapter 11. Deep and Shallow Copy - Cloning JavaScript Objects

In the journey of mastering JavaScript immutability, understanding the concept of copying objects is pivotal. In JavaScript, we are often required to duplicate objects, a task traditionally accomplished by either 'Shallow Copying' or 'Deep Copying'. Let's delve into the facets and profound implications of these techniques.

11.1. Understanding Shallow Copy

A Shallow copy of an object is a new object that holds the references to the original object's properties. When we say 'reference,' it suggests that any changes made to the original object's properties would exhibit in the cloned object. Take a look at the code snippet below:

```javascript
let originalObject = { key1: 'value1', key2: 'value2' };
let shallowClone = Object.assign({}, originalObject);
shallowClone.key1 = 'NewValue'; // Altering the property
in the cloned object.

console.log(originalObject.key1); // 'value1'
console.log(shallowClone.key1); // 'NewValue'
```

In this case, `Object.assign` was used to create a shallow copy of the originalObject. Despite changes to the shallowClone variable, the originalObject remained unaffected.

However, let's see what happens when our object contains not just primitives, but objects as well:

```javascript
let originalObject = {
  key1: 'value1',
  nestedObject: { nestedKey: 'nestedValue' }
};
let shallowClone = Object.assign({}, originalObject);
shallowClone.nestedObject.nestedKey = 'NewNestedValue';

console.log(originalObject.nestedObject.nestedKey);
//'NewNestedValue'
console.log(shallowClone.nestedObject.nestedKey);
//'NewNestedValue'
```

In this case, when the nested property inside the cloned object was changed, the same was reflected in the original object. Hence, for an object containing nested properties, a shallow copy might not be the best option.

11.2. The Spread Operator and Shallow Copying

The spread operator '...' is an alternative approach for performing a shallow copy in JavaScript. It essentially works in the same manner as `Object.assign()`. Its usage is as follows:

```javascript
let originalObject = { key1: 'value1', key2: 'value2' };
let shallowClone = { ...originalObject };
```

Just like in `Object.assign()`, if the object contains nested properties, its modifications will reflect on the original object.

11.3. Understanding Deep Copy

So what do we do when we need to clone an object with nested properties, and we don't want changes to the clone to reflect on the original object?

Enter Deep Copy. A Deep Copy fundamentally clones all values of the original object recursively, thereby producing an entirely independent copy of the object:

```javascript
let originalObject = {
  key1: 'value1',
  nestedObject: { nestedKey: 'nestedValue' }
};
let deepClone =
JSON.parse(JSON.stringify(originalObject));
deepClone.nestedObject.nestedKey = 'NewNestedValue';

console.log(originalObject.nestedObject.nestedKey);
//'nestedValue'
console.log(deepClone.nestedObject.nestedKey);
//'NewNestedValue'
```

In this case, the original object will remain unaffected by any changes made to the deepCloned object. We used the JSON.stringify() method to convert the original object into a string and then parsed it back to an object using JSON.parse(), creating a full copy of the object. This method works well for most cases; however, remember that it might not behave as expected for complex JavaScript objects.

11.4. Conclusion

In conclusion, the approach you use to clone an object in JavaScript deeply depends on your specific requirements. For simple JavaScript

objects without nested properties, a shallow copy using either
`Object.assign()` or the Spread operator suffices. On the other hand,
for objects with nested properties, deep copying is the better choice.
A solid understanding of these two techniques can largely enhance
your JavaScript technique and make the applications you create
more robust and effective.

Chapter 12. Manipulating JavaScript Arrays: The Immutable Way

JavaScript arrays represent a meaningful way of ordering items. Immutable operations ensure that rather than altering the original array, a brand new array is generated every time an operation is performed. Beyond preserving the integrity of your original data, this introduces predictability and improves debuggability in your applications. Harnessing immutability can seem daunting, especially when dealing with something as dynamic as JavaScript arrays. Still, using the right methods and understanding their behavior aids this task. Let's explore how to handle JavaScript Arrays in an immutable fashion.

12.1. Understanding Immutability

Immutability signifies unchangeability. For arrays, it means that once an array is created, it can't be changed by any operation. Manipulating an array leads to creating a new array, leaving the original one untouched. JavaScript, being a language with mutable array methods by default, doesn't support immutability out of the box.

Here's an example to depict a mutable operation:

```
let array1 = [1, 2, 3];
let array2 = array1;
array2.push(4);
console.log(array1); // [1, 2, 3, 4]
```

In this scenario, array1 is also modified when array2 is changed since they reference the same array. An immutable variant would look like:

```
let array1 = [1, 2, 3];
let array2 = [...array1];
array2.push(4);
console.log(array1); // [1, 2, 3]
console.log(array2); // [1, 2, 3, 4]
```

Here, array1 remains unchanged when array2 is transformed, thanks to the use of the spread syntax to copy array1. This is a simple introduction to immutability.

12.2. Immutable Array Manipulation Methods

We've different ways to ensure that array manipulations in JavaScript remain immutable. Let's examine each one in detail.

12.2.1. Adding Elements to an Array

JavaScript provides the push function to add a new item to an array. However, push mutates the original array. For an immutable operation, we use the concat function or the ES6 spread operator. Let's take a look.

Using concat

```
let array1 = [1, 2, 3];
let array2 = array1.concat(4);
console.log(array1); // [1, 2, 3]
console.log(array2); // [1, 2, 3, 4]
```

Using the spread operator

```
let array1 = [1, 2, 3];
let array2 = [...array1, 4];
console.log(array1); // [1, 2, 3]
console.log(array2); // [1, 2, 3, 4]
```

In both cases, array1 isn't affected when the new element is added to array2.

12.2.2. Removing Elements from an Array

Removing elements from an array in an immutable way can be achieved using the filter function. Here's an example:

```
let array1 = ["apple", "banana", "cherry"];
let array2 = array1.filter(item => item !== "banana");
console.log(array1); // ["apple", "banana", "cherry"]
console.log(array2); // ["apple", "cherry"]
```

array1 remains unchanged while array2 now houses the results.

12.2.3. Updating Elements in an Array

The map function provides a way to update elements in an array immutably. It creates a new array with the results of calling a provided function on every element in the array.

```
let array1 = [1, 2, 3];
let array2 = array1.map(item => item === 2 ? 20 : item);
console.log(array1); // [1, 2, 3]
console.log(array2); // [1, 20, 3]
```

The second array `array2` contains the updated value, whereas `array1` remains unchanged.

Chapter 13. Immutable Array Libraries

To facilitate working with immutable data structures, various libraries have emerged.

One notable library is Immutable.js by Facebook that provides many Persistent Immutable data structures including List, Stack, Map, OrderedMap, Set, OrderedSet and Record.

Another one is immutability-helper, a simple utility aiding in working with nested objects or arrays in JavaScript while preserving immutability.

These libraries provide rich APIs to work with arrays or objects immutably, but they introduce new syntax and a learning curve. For simpler use-cases, native JavaScript array functions like `concat`, `filter`, and `map` or operators like ⋯ (spread) work just fine.

Chapter 14. Conclusion

In conclusion, manipulating JavaScript arrays the immutable way brings about predictable results, improves performance, and renders debugging easier. With the advantages it offers, it's worthwhile mastering this skill. Training ourselves to use immutable patterns today will save us countless debugging hours. Remember, every new operation yields a fresh new array, leaving the original array unchanged. Of course, for more complex scenarios where nested objects are involved, libraries like Immutable.js can be a real timesaver. Nonetheless, the native array manipulation functions– `map`, `filter`, `concat`, or ES6 spread operators– are often sufficient to meet most needs. Happy coding!

Chapter 15. Exploring Immutable.js: An Introduction

Immutable.js is a library developed by Facebook to facilitate working with immutable collections in JavaScript. Rather than manipulating objects directly, Immutable.js employs a new approach of treating each modification as a new instance, preserving the original state and facilitating tracking throughout your codebase.

`Immutable.js` embraces two abstract data types that are cornerstones of functional programming: persistent data structures and lazy sequences.

15.1. Understanding Immutable Data Structures

Immutable data structures are structures that do not change once they are created. In JavaScript, we are accustomed to working with mutable data structures, where we can change a property of an object or add items to an array. Contrarily, with immutable structures, the concept of "change" is non-existent.

Let's have an example for our better understanding:

```
let mutableArray = [1, 2, 3];
mutableArray.push(4); // mutableArray is now [1, 2, 3, 4]
```

Here, we can clearly see that we've modified mutableArray. In an immutable scenario, we would create a new array without modifying the original one:

```
let immutableArray = Immutable.List([1, 2, 3]);
let newArray = immutableArray.push(4);
// immutableArray remains as [1, 2, 3]
// while newArray is [1, 2, 3, 4]
```

15.2. The Need for Persistence

Persistence, in the context of computing science, is the property of data outliving the process that created it.

Consider the scenario mentioned before: when we `push` a value into `mutableArray`, it also affects all other variables referencing `mutableArray`. This creates a problem of unnecessary mutations that might not be trackable. Thus, persistent data structures are favored in functional programming due to their predictability factor.

15.3. Using Persistent Data Structures in Immutable.js

Immutable.js encourages a function programming paradigm that rewards the careful handling of data. As such, its core is shaped by persistent data structures.

To create a persistent data structure in immutable.js, we use the following:

```
let list1 = Immutable.List([0, 1, 2, 3, 4, 5]);
let list2 = list1.push(6);
console.log(list1.toArray()); // [0, 1, 2, 3, 4, 5]
console.log(list2.toArray()); // [0, 1, 2, 3, 4, 5, 6]
```

Despite pushing a value onto our original list (list1), the original list remains unchanged while a new list (list2) with the added value is created.

15.4. Immutable API Deep Dive

One of the strengths of Immutable.js is its rich API. It provides a variety of data structures you can use, such as: List, Stack, Map, OrderedMap, Set, OrderedSet and Record. Note that all structures are used in a similar way. You create a new instance by calling the constructor and use dot notation to access the methods.

The following table details the available data structures and their corresponding descriptions:

Data Structure	Description
List	Efficient immutable indexed array implementation
Stack	Efficient immutable stack implementation (last in, first out)
Map	Unordered Keyed collections
OrderedMap	Ordered collections of key-value pairs
Set	Unordered collections of unique elements
OrderedSet	Ordered set of unique values
Record	Creates a class with a specified shape, similar to an object but immutable

15.5. Embracing Lazy Sequences

A Lazy sequence (Seq) is an Immutable.js data structure that allows a collection of values to be computed on-demand, not upfront. This helps in improving efficiency in cases where you don't need to process all data at once but only require a select few to be processed, all the while maintaining immutability.

To demonstrate, consider an array with a million items. If you wanted to transform all of these items, it would take time. But with Seq, transformations are lazy and are only computed when they are needed.

```
let oneToAMillion = Immutable.Range(1, 1000001);
let lazySeq = oneToAMillion.map(x => x * x).take(5);
console.log(lazySeq.toArray()); // [1, 4, 9, 16, 25]
```

In this example, we set up a sequence to map and take the first five elements. But in reality, only the first five elements are ever calculated.

15.6. Conclusion

Getting started with Immutable.js might seem daunting, but once you've mastered its principles, your code will be more predictable and easier to debug. By taking control of your data and replacing mutation with persistence, you're able to make your applications more scalable and maintainable.

This chapter introduced the fundamental concepts of Immutable.js, providing you with the groundwork required to harness its power. It showcases that JavaScript's flexible nature allows for the fusion of diverse paradigms, making your journey all the more exciting.

So, keep exploring, keep coding, and remember: always favour immutability!

Chapter 16. Beyond Basic Operations with Immutable.js

Before we delve into Immutable.js's more intricate operations, it's crucial to understand the library's foundational concepts. Immutable.js, a library introduced by Facebook, focuses on providing persistent, immutable collections in JavaScript. These collections once created, never change, promoting predictable behavior and traceability in your code.

16.1. Understanding Persistent Data Structures

It's essential to distinguish the concept of persistence in data structures. In an ephemeral data structure (like most JavaScript objects), alterations modify that specific instance. However, persistent data structures, like those provided by Immutable.js, generate new instances when modified, preserving original instances intact. This characteristic is critical for achieving predictability and traceability in applications.

16.2. Immutability vs. Performance

A valid question arises: If new instances are created upon every change, does it not gobble up memory? At first glance, it might seem so. However, Immutable.js uses structural sharing, which allows new and old instances to share common parts, generating only altered parts. This technique conservationally uses memory and ensures excellent performance.

Let's traverse the path to deeper understanding by covering some intermediate operations in Immutable.js.

16.3. Map Merges

Immutable.js introduces the concept of a Map, an immutable equivalent of JavaScript's object or dictionary. The `merge` method allows two Maps to be combined, with the second one overwriting the same keys in the first if they occur.

```
const map1 = Immutable.Map({ a: 1, b: 2, c: 3 });
const map2 = Immutable.Map({ b: 50, c: 100, d: 150 });
const mergedMap = map1.merge(map2);
console.log(mergedMap.toJS()); // { a: 1, b: 50, c: 100,
d: 150 }
```

Note the use of `.toJS()` method here. It conveniently converts Immutable.js's Maps and other collections into native JavaScript objects for debugging or display.

16.4. List Concatenation

In addition to Maps, Immutable.js introduces the concept of Lists. Lists are like arrays, but, as the name suggests, immutable. Lists have a `concat` method analogous to JavaScript's array `concat`, allowing you to join multiple lists into a single one.

```
const list1 = Immutable.List([1, 2, 3]);
const list2 = Immutable.List([4, 5, 6]);
const concatenatedList = list1.concat(list2);
console.log(concatenatedList.toJS()); // [1, 2, 3, 4, 5,
6]
```

Like with Maps, we use the `.toJS()` method to convert the Immutable.js List into a native JavaScript array.

16.5. Intermediate Data Transformations

Immutable.js provides a plethora of sophisticated methods to manipulate and transform collections.

The `map` method behaves similarly to its JavaScript array counterpart, transforming each value in a collection based on a provided function.

```
const list = Immutable.List([1, 2, 3]);
const transformedList = list.map(x => x * 10);
console.log(transformedList.toJS()); // [10, 20, 30]
```

The `filter` method, akin to JavaScript's native method, creates a new collection containing elements satisfying a condition.

```
const list = Immutable.List([1, 2, 3, 4, 5, 6]);
const filteredList = list.filter(x => x % 2 === 0);
console.log(filteredList.toJS()); // [2, 4, 6]
```

The `reduce` method allows aggregating collection elements into a single value, similar to JavaScript's array `reduce`.

```
const list = Immutable.List([1, 2, 3, 4, 5]);
const sum = list.reduce((acc, value) => acc + value, 0);
console.log(sum); // 15
```

16.6. Sequences for Laziness

Utilizing laziness, Immutable.js promotes efficiency by creating intermediary "sequences" to perform compound operations. Unlike immediately transformed collections, Sequences defer execution until necessary, dramatically boosting effectiveness in large data manipulations.

```javascript
const list = Immutable.List([1, 2, 3, 4, 5, 6, 7, 8, 9,
10]);
const lazySeq = list
  .map(x => x * 2)
  .filter(x => x > 10)
  .take(4);
console.log(lazySeq.toJS()); // [12, 14, 16, 18]
```

Here, `take(4)` implies only the first four numbers are required. Hence, only necessary computations are performed.

16.7. Additional resources

Remember, Immutable.js is an expansive library and we've scratched just the surface. Visit Facebook's GitHub repository to explore comprehensive documentation and engage with the vibrant developer community. Keep practicing and applying this robust library to gain mastery in applying JavaScript immutability.

In summary, Immutable.js provides a rich set of immutable data structures and intermediate-transformative methods to empower JavaScript developers. Embracing these facilities can make your application's state management more predictable, testable, and easier to debug - an essential tool for modern-day JavaScript development.

Chapter 17. How Immutability Leads to More Predictable Code

In the context of programming, immutability refers to the property that data cannot be changed once created. That is, an immutable object, once created, always retains its initial state. It's an influential paradigm, having substantial effects on software development, including how we model, write, and reason about our code. In JavaScript, immutability can lead to a more predictable, easier-to-understand codebase. Here's how:

17.1. The Principle of Immutability

Immutable data structures cannot be altered once created. This entails any modification, addition, or removal of elements results in a new data structure, leaving the original untouched. In JavaScript, we often use const to declare immutable variables. However, `const` merely prevents reassignment; the declared object or array can still be mutated. Hence, we employ methods like `Object.freeze()` or third-party libraries such as Immutable.js to achieve true immutability.

Practically, immutability results in a codebase where functions safely operate on data without side effects, freeing the developers from having to track changes to state over time. Because the state cannot change after its creation, errors due to mutation or timing (race conditions) are eliminated. Software is made modular, manageable, and significantly more predictable.

17.2. Advantages of Immutability

Let's delve deeper into how immutability leads to more predictable code:

- **Predictability:** Immutable objects maintain their state, thus eliminating the risks of unexpected mutation. Developers can interact with data confidently, knowing it won't change behind the scenes. This can greatly simplify debugging, testing, and reasoning about code.

- **Simpler Code:** Immutability eliminates side effects, where data changes unexpectedly. This can considerably simplify your code by allowing functions to be safely isolated from the rest of the system.

- **Performance Enhancements:** Immutability allows for performance optimizations such as memoization. A result can be cached and reused if the function is called again with the same parameters, as the function will always yield the same output.

- **Concurrency:** Immutable objects are inherently thread-safe because they can't be changed once they're created, reducing bugs and complexity in multithreaded code.

17.3. Working With Immutable State

To demonstrate the practical application of immutability in JavaScript, consider the following scenario. A function `addItem()` takes a list and an item, and returns the list with the item added. Despite appearing simple, if implemented carelessly, it could introduce bugs stemming from mutable state.

```javascript
// Mutating version
const addItem = (list, item) => {
    list.push(item);
    return list;
};

const originalList = [1, 2, 3];
```

```javascript
const modifiedList = addItem(originalList, 4);

console.log(originalList); // [1, 2, 3, 4]
console.log(modifiedList); // [1, 2, 3, 4]
```

In the above example, `originalList` is unexpectedly mutated. This could lead to a host of issues, especially as the codebase grows and multiple parts of the application may depend on `originalList` maintaining its initial state.

To eliminate these concerns, revise the `addItem()` function to create and return a new list, leaving the original unaltered.

```javascript
// Immutable version
const addItem = (list, item) => {
    return [...list, item];
};

const originalList = [1, 2, 3];
const modifiedList = addItem(originalList, 4);

console.log(originalList); // [1, 2, 3]
console.log(modifiedList); // [1, 2, 3, 4]
```

The immutable version of `addItem()` is predictable, directly enhancing code sustainability by maintaining `originalList`'s initial state.

17.4. Deep Immutability

When dealing with nested object structures or arrays, we need to ensure immutability at all levels, known as deep immutability. Unfortunately, JavaScript does not offer built-in deep immutability, we need to use recursion or a library that supports it, such as

Immutable.js or lodash's `_.cloneDeep()` function.

17.5. Immutable.js

Immutable.js is a library providing persistent immutable data structures. Persistent data structures reuse as much of the existing structure as possible when creating a new one, yielding efficiency and simplicity of state change handling. Immutable.js enhances JavaScript with a powerful suite of data structures and methods for manipulating them immutably.

Ultimately, thoroughly implementing immutability simplifies software architecture, enhances system integrity, makes code easier to maintain and reason about, and in turn, contributes to more predictable code. Deriving these benefits requires a shift in thought patterns and a solid grasp of immutability-aligned libraries, but the pay-off is certainly worth the investment. It's a skill that will change how you develop software for the better, promising robust, maintainable, efficient, and reliable applications.

Chapter 18. Immutability and React: Best Practices

JavaScript's functionality and flexibility make it one of the most widely used programming languages globally. In particular, its potential for building versatile user interfaces is harnessed by the popular JavaScript library, React. This report delves into the crucial aim of achieving immutability patterns within the context of a React-powered environment.

18.1. Understanding Immutability

Immutability, as the name suggests, denotes data that cannot be changed once created. To modify any piece of data, a new instance must instead be created. This aspect becomes critical when dealing with complex applications, particularly those requiring synchronous and concurrent operations, making efficient debugging and predicting potential changes a must. Achieving immutability patterns in JavaScript is essential, and React encourages this concept for a smoother state management and performance improvements.

18.2. The Need for Immutability in React

Immutability is at the core of pure functions, or functions whose return values are determined solely by their input and cause no side effects. However, JavaScript objects and arrays are mutable by default. Consequently, careful management is required to maintain immutability and prevent unnecessary component re-renders caused by accidental mutations.

React incorporates a diffing algorithm that compares the current

DOM with a new one to identify the minimal updates needed for re-rendering. Immutable data can provide improved performance here by allowing React to quickly compare old and new props and state. If no changes are detected, React can skip re-rendering the component entirely, thereby saving rendering time.

18.3. Best Practices for Achieving Immutability in React

The following sections suggest methods and best practices to enforce immutability in your React applications, ensuring more reliable, efficient, and maintainable code.

18.3.1. Avoid Directly Modifying State

The state should never be altered directly in React. Instead, `this.setState()` or `useState` hook (for functional components) should always be used. This is because direct modifications to the state wouldn't trigger an update, leading to potential inconsistencies within the application.

18.3.2. Clone Objects and Arrays Before Modifying

Most JavaScript objects and arrays are mutable by default. Thus, care should be taken to avoid mutational operations. Here's where the concept of cloning comes into play. For instance, let's illustrate this with JavaScript arrays:

```
let originalArray = [1, 2, 3, 4, 5];
let newArray = [...originalArray]; // an ES6 method of cloning
newArray[0] = 100;
```

In this case, newArray is a cloned copy of originalArray, shielding originalArray from changes to newArray.

18.3.3. Use Immutability Helpers

Given the importance of maintaining immutability in React, several libraries are available to help enforce this. Some popular libraries include Immutable.js and Immer, both of which aid in dealing with nested objects and providing handy functions.

Immer, for instance, provides a `produce` function that allows developers to work with a draftState (a copy of the original state) and automatically apply updates in an immutable manner:

```
import produce from "immer";

let state = {value: 1};

let newState = produce(state, draftState => {
  draftState.value++;
});
```

In this example, newState is a new, immutable object, and changes to value in newState have no effect on state.

18.3.4. Leverage Pure Components

Another way to enforce immutability is by taking advantage of React's PureComponent. A PureComponent performs a shallow comparison of props and state in its `shouldComponentUpdate()` lifecycle method, achieving significant performance gains if your data remains primarily immutable.

18.4. Conclusion

Enhancing your JavaScript and React codebase to enforce immutability can help deliver improved predictability, easier debugging, and performance gains. Maintain good practices such as cloning before modifying and using immutability helper libraries, and your React applications will bask in the benefits of immutability. Tomorrow's application architecture needs today's rock-solid foundation. Get future-ready with immutability, and reconceptualize your coding prowess.

Chapter 19. Real-world Applications: Case Studies on Immutability Patterns

Immutability, in programming, is about establishing data that can't be changed. JavaScript, traditionally, doesn't enforce immutability on its data types or objects. However, we can achieve immutability in JavaScript through certain patterns and practices, which can bring along benefits such as readability, maintainability, and predictability. Through this chapter, we will explore several real-world applications and case studies on how immutability patterns improve JavaScript applications.

19.1. Understanding Mutable and Immutable Data

Data in JavaScript can be divided into two categories: mutable and immutable. Mutable data can be changed after it's created, while immutable data cannot. For instance, JavaScript's primitives (excluding `null` and `undefined`) are all immutable. They do not hold any state that can change. When you make a change to a variable that is a primitive, you are creating a new primitive and assigning it to that variable.

On the other hand, objects and arrays are mutable in JavaScript. They hold state that can be changed, and when that state is changed, it modifies the original object or array. This can lead to difficulties in tracking where and when data is altered, leading to confusing bugs and challenges in code maintainability.

19.2. Unintended Consequences of Mutation

Before we delve into our case studies, let's understand the implications of mutability. In JavaScript, objects and arrays are passed by reference. This means if you create an object (or array), assign it to another variable and then make changes through any of them, it will affect all of them.

This is an important fact because it can sometimes lead to unexpected bugs. For instance, you might inadvertently mutate global state from within a function, leading to code that behaves unexpectedly or is difficult to debug.

Say you have an array of items representing a shopping basket:

```
let basket = ["Apple", "Banana", "Cherry"];
```

And you have a function that adds an item:

```
function addItem(item) {
  basket.push(item);
}
```

Although this function seems straightforward, it has a side effect: it alters the original basket array. If another part of your code relies on the unchanged basket array, it will behave incorrectly.

19.3. Immutable Patterns in JavaScript

So how can we avoid mutations and implement immutability in

JavaScript? There are a few strategies we can apply.

1. Using const: The const keyword can be used to prevent reassignment of variable identifiers. However, this doesn't make objects or arrays immutable.

2. Spread / Rest operators: Introduced in ES6, the spread (for arrays) and rest (for objects) operators allow us to create copies of arrays and objects which we can then modify, ensuring the original data remains unaltered.

3. Virtual Copies with Object.freeze(): This method prevents modification of properties in objects (shallow immutability).

4. Using Libraries: Libraries like Immutable.js allow for complete immutation of data, including nested objects and arrays.

Let's explore a few case studies where immutability has improved the implementation and functionality of real-world applications.

19.4. Case Study 1: Streamlining eCommerce Transactions

In a global eCommerce company, there was continual difficulty tracking and debugging orders as they moved through various stages. A key issue was the mutation of the original order object as it moved from one process to another such as processing, packing, and shipping, which sometimes led to conflicts and bugs.

With the introduction of immutability in the application, an order object was made immutable as soon as it was created. Then, each subsequent process would generate a new order object with the changes needed without affecting the original one. Not only did this make it easier to track progress and changes, but it also reduced the number of concurrency conflicts that occurred.

19.5. Case Study 2: Simplifying State Management in Social Media App

A popular social media application encountered problems in debugging and tracking user activities, given the constant alterations in the application's global state.

Through incorporating immutability patterns, each action on the app now creates a new state without mutating the existing state. This pattern, used in conjunction with libraries such as Redux, improved the debugging process since it was now easier to identify the specific actions that led to the current state.

19.6. Case Study 3: Stable Game States in a Multiplayer Online Game

A browser-based multiplayer online game had to maintain various clients with different game states. Numerous synchronization issues arose from mutating these states.

With the introduction of immutability patterns, every move a player made resulted in a new but identical game board state. This way, all players' boards could be synchronized without losing their individual step states, leading to a smoother, more stable user experience.

19.7. Case Study 4: Predictability in Financial Data Handling

A financial technology company, dealing with sensitive financial data, introduced immutable patterns to their data handling module. This resulted in predictable operations and reduced the chance of accidental data modifications—an extremely crucial aspect in the finance domain.

19.8. Takeaways

In JavaScript, while mutable data comes with flexibility, it also brings potential bugs and harder to track issues. Immutable patterns can offer predictability, easier debugging, and improved understanding of data flow in complex applications. While JavaScript does not enforce immutability innately, patterns and practices can be leveraged to bring about immutability and improve our applications. Exploring the real-world application of these patterns illustrates the impact and power of immutability in the JavaScript world.